Jellybean Books™

A Child's
BOOK of HOPE

By **Jean Monrad Thomas**
Illustrated by **Mary Haverfield**

Random House 🏠 New York

Library of Congress Catalog Card Number: 97-68539
ISBN 0-679-88617-6 (trade) ; 0-679-98617-0 (lib. bdg.)

www.randomhouse.com/kids

Printed in the United States of America   10 9 8 7 6 5 4 3 2 1
JELLYBEAN BOOKS is a trademark of Random House, Inc.

*H*ope *can be found*
In a tiny seed,
Or a fat bulb
Hidden in the ground.
They have their own secrets—
They know what they will be.

There they lie, small, dry,
Apparently dead; yet
Waiting only for sun and rain
And the right moment in time—

To spring into life!
Mountain Columbine,
Transparent with morning dew,
Pale sapphire petals over
Lacy yellow petticoat,
Heads hung shyly down.

And stately Amaryllis,
Its fiery triple crown
Standing guard
Along the garden wall.

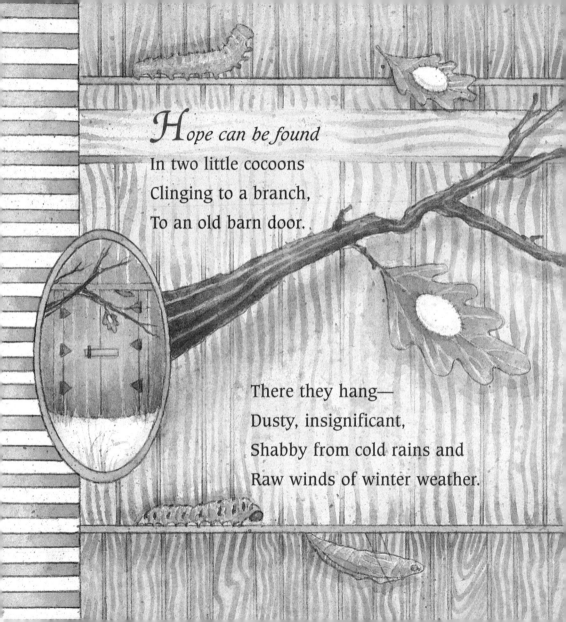

*H*ope can be found
In two little cocoons
Clinging to a branch,
To an old barn door.

There they hang—
Dusty, insignificant,
Shabby from cold rains and
Raw winds of winter weather.

They have their own secrets—
They know what they will be.
For hidden inside lie
Two caterpillars, waiting,
Waiting, changing—
Ready at last to break
Out of their prisons—

Into the warm spring air!
One a lovely Luna Moth
With fur-covered body
And delicate, luminous
Long-tailed wings.

And one a handsome butterfly
Called Giant Swallowtail,
Its slender body dressed
In the brown and yellow
Splendor of its wings.

*H*ope can be found
In two fat tadpoles
Darting here and there
In the shallows of a pond.
Do they guess
Their comical secret?
Or are they astonished when—

*T*heir legs pop out,
Their tails disappear,
And they discover—

*L*ittle toad, little frog—
That they are
Not little fishes after all!

*H*ope can be found
In all newborn things.

Wet-feathered chick,
All tuckered out
Pecking its way from cozy egg
To have a first look
At the world.

Or lively little colt
Struggling to balance
On faltering legs—and then
Out and away in the meadow!

*A*nd hope can be found
In a child,
A girl or boy.

They have a special secret
Belonging to no other creature
In the world.

They can choose
How they will be.
Choose to be kind.
Choose to be fair and just.
Choose to dream.

Choose to love
And trust in
Being loved.